Effective Money Habits

Marcella Sersante

Copyright

© Copyright 2021 Marcella Sersante

All Rights Reserved

Protected with www.protectmywork.com

Reference Number: 13213040821S009

Table of Contents

Introduction — 5

Chapter 1 — 7
What are habits? — 7
How do habits form? — 9
Identifying bad habits — 11
Breaking a habit — 12
Building a new habit — 14

Chapter 2 — 16
Bad money habits — 16
Examples of bad money habits — 18

Chapter 3 — 23
Spending more than you earn — 23
Going overdraft — 28
Impulse buying — 30
Not setting money aside — 32
You do not have a financial plan — 35
You don't shop around — 37
You live above your means — 38

Chapter 4 — 42
You are not sticking to a budget — 42
You are not paying off your credit card in full each month — 45
Making late payments — 48
Spending too much on groceries — 50
You are buying everything new — 52
You are overloaded with subscription services — 54

You are buying lunch everyday | 55

Chapter 5 | **57**

Taking payday loans | 57

You have a consumer mentality | 61

Worrying about impressing others | 63

Relying on credit to pay bills | 65

Not taking control of your career | 67

Not educating yourself about personal finance | 70

Not spending wisely | 73

Chapter 6 | **75**

Good money habits | 75

Get on a budget | 76

The 50/20/30 budget rule. | 79

Live below your means | 80

Pay off debt | 84

Automate your finances | 89

Build your emergency fund | 91

Chapter 7 | **94**

Grow your money by investing | 94

Get there right insurance | 100

Conserve your utilities | 108

Increase your income | 112

Conclusion | **115**

Other Books By the Author | **116**

Introduction

We all have habits we adopt throughout our lives. Some of them are good for us and some of them not so much.

Habits are present in several facets of our lives, including on our finances. You have developed behaviors that shape how you deal with money. Some of them take years to form, and as such, you execute them without much deliberation.

Some of the habits are not generating a positive outcome, and these are the ones you want to change. For that to happen, you need to be analytical and be able to see the behavior, how it gets triggered and what the outcome is.

If you really want to change the outcome, then you will have to change the behavior. Otherwise, you will be getting the same results over and over again.

What is your financial goal? How are you going to get there? It is an important starting point to know where you want to go and identifying what is preventing you from getting where you want to be.

Breaking habits is not easy. Your natural instinct will be to resist the changes after all that you have been doing is familiar. Keep the focus on what you want to achieve to find the motivation to make necessary changes that can have a massive impact on your life.

You have an opportunity to alter the course of your life, make positive changes, and reap positive results. Isn't that worth it?

Start small, make some changes and then keep an eye on the end result. It might be slow, it might be painful, but you will get there!

Chapter 1

What are habits?

If you think, you can probably identify some of the habits you practice every day. The small decisions you make, the actions you perform so often that you are no longer even aware you are doing them. You are performing these actions without much of a conscious decision on your part. You go a little bit on autopilot, and that can be a bad thing. You lose awareness.

According to Dr. Gardner (from King's College London), 'habit works by generating an impulse to do a behavior with little or no conscious thought.' Forming a habit releases the brain to do other things.

A behavior that requires effort or concentration is not a habit and with a habit, not doing a behavior feels somehow wrong, and you feel bad.

Some of these behaviors can prevent you from attaining your goals. Your actions will typically have a short-term reward feeling, so you feel instant gratification and cannot see its true effects in the longer term.

Not all habits are bad. Some are a necessity and provide you with good outcomes. The danger lies when you stop noticing the results of your actions in relation to your goals in life. The danger of not stopping and analyzing your results and giving the first steps in the direction of change.

Scientists have learned that a specific part of the brain called ganglia plays a role in creating new habits and maintaining existing ones. That is why after significant brain damage, people will still do certain things they've always done before. These people often don't even know how or why they can still do certain things.

Before the behavior, you will have a trigger. Once the trigger happens, you exhibit the behavior, and then you achieve the result. How the result makes you feel reinforces behaviors. The reward is an immediate reward, so it is a lot easier to give in to an ingrained habit.

Being able to identify the triggers is the key to understanding your habits and having a chance to alter them.

In terms of rewards, having a short-term reward that you can experience now seems preferable to one you need to wait for. That is why having a long-term focus rather than a short-term one is necessary. You are not looking for satisfaction now, but rather a better outcome in the future. Understanding this will help you fight the short-term reward addition.

How do habits form?

According to research (Ouellette and Wood, 1998) on habit formation, behavior is likely to become habitual when frequently and consistently performed in the same context.

Habits are our brain's way of increasing its efficiency. Daily actions and behaviors are turned into habits by our brain so that we would do them automatically and without too much thought.

The first time you do something, it requires a lot of your concentration and brainpower. But as you repeat it, it becomes easier. The mental power you need to perform these tasks decreases significantly.

Habits form by trigger, repetition, and reward. Basically, that translates to learning, repetition, and rewards.

A behavior, through regular repetition, becomes automatic or habitual.

Internal or external stress can trigger habits to develop unconsciously. These tend to be negative.

Another critical aspect of forming a habit is to have positive reinforcement or reward. For an activity to become a habit, it helps if it is repeated often and positively reinforced.

We can trigger positive reinforcement through an external reward, like money, food, or praise. Such experiences release dopamine, one of the brain's favorite feel-good neurochemicals.

How long it will take a person to learn a new habit is dependent on the habit in question. A 2009 study highlighted a range of variables in habit-forming that make it impossible to establish a one-size-fits-all.

Ingrained habits would automatically arise in the face of solid cues associated with their formation.

Certain habits take longer to form, and some people are better suited to forming habits than others. Many studies suggest that it takes, on average, more than two months before a new behavior becomes automatic.

If you are trying to form new habits, beware that it can take you less time or even longer. Do not get down on yourself. Just be persistent.

Identifying bad habits

This may sound obvious, but the first way to address and overcome a bad habit is to become aware there is a problem. This sounds simple, but it can be one of the most difficult steps.

You will need to analyze your actions. You need to identify what the problem is and then look to see what is causing it. If it is easier for you, write them down.

It makes sense to conclude that if you want different results, then you will need to change paths or directions in life.

You won't achieve a different result if you keep doing what you have been doing all along. You will get the same results you were getting before.

Change is difficult for most people, as you have to get out of your comfort zone. Some people might resist it, leading us never to change what we do.

You are looking to identify the underlying cause behind your bad habit. By becoming aware and acknowledging the issues, you are then giving the first steps in the right direction.

If something is not working for you, identify the behavior behind it. You need to be able to come out of the auto-pilot mode and be able to determine what results you are achieving versus what you want to achieve.

Only when you are intentionally aware of your actions will you be able to affect the outcome by changing your behavior in the first place.

Once you identify the bad habit, consider what you have to change to achieve the desired outcome. Start by practicing the new behavior. Remember, repetition is the key. When you reach your goal, that will be an even better incentive for you to repeat the cue in the first place.

The reward will be short-term in principle but consider what you can achieve in the long run by changing your actions now. Your aim has to be long-term in order to achieve consistent results.

Breaking a habit

All of your current habits - good or bad- are in your life for a reason. These behaviors provide some perceived or real benefit to you. You need to decide what category they fit in.

Acknowledging you have bad habits is not enough: you need to know what behaviors you want to change.

By understanding how you make decisions is the key to conquering all kinds of bad habits, including the ones related to money. What triggers for you a specific behavior? How can you stop it?

One option is to replace one habit with another, a healthier one which will bring you the required results. Keep an eye on long-term results. It might not give you instant satisfaction, but it might contribute to a healthier financial outcome later on, and that can only be positive.

Consider why you want to change. It might be easier to change your behavior when the change you want to make is valuable or beneficial to you.

It is possible you might slip up. This is normal. Breaking a habit can be challenging, and it is very easy to slip back into old patterns than fighting to stick to new ones. You need to know that it takes a while to build up a new habit. Don't be discouraged.

Having a clear goal to where you want to be heading is the key to keep your focus on the right place.

It takes time and effort to form better habits, and breaking established bad habits will be even harder to do. So be patient with yourself and try focusing on one habit and the smallest steps you can take.

For your brain to form new connections and a new behavior pattern to kick in, it will take a while.

By repeating the same behaviors in the same place, your surroundings can become a trigger. Switch up your surroundings in even the slightest way as this might interfere with your trigger, and therefore it will help you to introduce changes.

Building a new habit

Good habits happen when you set yourself up for success. You are looking at the long-term results.

The easiest way to form a new habit is to tie it to an existing habit. You would have a better chance of creating a new habit of an existing one than creating one from scratch.

Start small. Start with tiny habits to make the new habit as easy as possible in the beginning. If needed, break the habit into various components so you can tackle them one at a time and will have time to adapt.

Don't divide your attention and energy among too many new habits, especially not early on.

Keep it regular. It can take time for habits to form, but they form faster when we do them more often.

If it helps, track your behaviors, in the beginning so you ensure that after the cue, you are actually following the new behavior rather than falling into what you are used to.

Having greater awareness of our habits - the good and the bad - and constructing new pathways in the brain will inform us how we conduct ourselves in our lives. With this knowledge and a few strategic choices, we can maintain those habits that serve us well and change those that don't.

Evaluate your progress often. This is a good tool as you can see if you are getting with the schedule or if you would need some more time to adapt. If you are finding it difficult, you might want to break it even further.

Never miss twice. Be prepared for a lip-up. How are you going to redirect your course? Is there anyone who can help you? The key is to identify a slip-up and then get back on track immediately so that you aim to never miss twice.

Don't allow an exception. There is no place for excuses. Keep focused.

Reward yourself. Each time you reward yourself, you reaffirm and reinforce the behavior, and after all that hard work, you will deserve it.

Chapter 2

Bad money habits

There are many aspects of your financial situation that you can control; getting rid of bad money habits and forming new, responsible ones for spending and borrowing can set you up for success.

To help you break bad money habits, it is essential to set a specific financial goal. What do you want to achieve? How are you going to get there?

You have to know where you want to go, as this is the key to maintaining the right path towards your goal. If you do not have that clear, how are you going to achieve it? You can't work towards something you do not know you want to achieve.

Having a goal, an objective, will help you achieve things faster as you focus on making them a reality.

If you do not have any savings and spend more than you earn, it is time to drop the bad habits and start working towards better financial practices. Take control of your finances.

Creating good money habits can increase wealth and set you up for financial success. This will also help you understand how to budget, save money, and work towards your financial goals.

It won't be quick, but with persistence and know-how, you can start the change.

You have to change your current mindset in order to build wealth. As your everyday spending habits change, so will your overall financial situation. With some discipline and action, you can make a few good money habits into your day that will positively impact your economic life.

Changes in how you have been doing things are essential. Otherwise, nothing will happen.

You will never have control over your money if you don't know where it is going. Awareness is important. Having your priorities clear will help you avoid impulse buying and stick to your saving goals.

That type of clarity will help you focus on being deliberate when you plan and when you spend.

Are you aware of your spending habits? You spend the same way with the same set of conditions. Because it is a habit, it may be so natural and involuntary that you don't even realize what you are doing.

We are used to how we spend and save. The challenge is creating a new normal. That involves mindset and, consequently, behavioral changes.

The key is to understand what, why, and how you have been spending—examining all these facets so you can then put things into context. You can't change what you don't know.

Analyzing your financial patterns can be scary and even daunting, but this discomfort will be worthwhile because, without that, you will not indicate what needs to be changed.

Examples of bad money habits

Take a look at your finances. What do they look like? What can you do to improve it?

Are you able to identify what habits are not helping you to get there? What are their cues?

Being aware of your actions is the first step in changing. Try to identify which ones you will need to work on.

Find below some examples of bad money habits:

- **Spending more than you earn.** You constantly struggle to have money on your account, especially towards the end of the month.

- **Going overdraft.** You might have had unexpected costs coming up, and yo've had no choice but to use your overdraft. You might be using your overdraft every month to survive. The bank is charging you because of it, which will make it even harder to get out of your current situation.

- **Impulse buying**. If you see something you like, you go ahead and buy it. If you don't have the money, you put it on credit. You canâ€™t resist certain items. You reason that there is no point in saving up when you could buy it now and pay it off later. It means you don't always have money when you need it.

- **Not having an emergency fund.** You are not regularly setting money aside. You spend all your paycheck, and therefore there is nothing left to keep. You are not prepared for any emergency, and any extra cost will push you even further into debt.

- **Not shopping around**. If you look at something and you like it, you buy it right then. You are not interested in shopping around.

As a result, you often miss spotting things cheaper somewhere else.

- **You don't have a budget.** If you do not have a budget, you can't know how much you have got to spend, which will allow you to overspend and not even know it. This is the most basic and vital item you need to have. How do you know how much you can spend each month while still living within your means?

- **Carrying a balance forward on your credit card each month.** You pay the minimum amount due as it is not a lot each month. If you are not paying in full, then the interest will be rolling over and over each month. Soon that minimum amount won't be cheap anymore. Credit cards can quickly turn into a significant debt burden if you are not careful.

- **Making late payments**. They can have lasting consequences when it comes to your credit score and your wallet.

- **Spending too much on groceries** It is easy to spend more than you mean at the grocery store. Always use a list of what you need and stick to it.

- **Buying everything new.** You do not need to buy everything new all the time. You can save hundreds of dollars each year.

- **Having too many subscription services.** It is easy to sign up for a subscription and forget about it. Keep the ones you need. Ditch the rest.

- **Not having set financial goals** You need to have a goal so that all the budgeting and saving have a reason to be. If you do not have a destination in mind, you can't get to where you want to be. You will be distracted on your way, and as you do not have a destination, you will be lost.

- **Buying lunch every day.** It is just easy to buy lunch/drinks. They have small costs. If you calculate how much you are spending a year, you will see that it will all add up. The more food you prepare at home, the better off your food budget will be.

- **Taking out payday loans**. You need extra cash for emergencies or to live day by day. Payday loans seem easy but beware; they are one of the worst forms of debt.

- **Have a consumer mentality.** Your primary focus is to buy things as you are always looking at ads and social media and believe that this will be the key to your happiness. You never stop to think if you need that item in your life, it seems interesting and fashionable, so this is all you need to know.

- **Worrying about impressing others**. Making this your priority is a sure way to stay broke. You constantly worry about what others have and try to impress them with material things. If the neighbor has bought a new car, you then need to consider upgrading yours too, right? Your friend has got the latest phone. You start looking at yours and think maybe it is time for you to change it too.

- **Living on credit.** Not taking a car loan or a new credit card may be easy, but saving up enough to buy a house is more complicated. If you try to get a mortgage without a credit score, you will have to undergo manual underwriting, which will carry some requirements. Depending on your credit history, negative marks typically stay on your credit report for seven to 10 years.

- **Hiding from your money issues**. Ignoring your money issues will not make them go away. If you live on credit and spend more than you earn, stop hiding, address the problem, and get it sorted. Ignoring the situation won't make it go away magically. You need to start taking responsibility for your choices.

Chapter 3

Spending more than you earn

You get your paycheck, and it all magically disappears! To keep up with the lifestyle you are accustomed to, there is t no other option but to dip into your savings, borrow, and use credit.

If you stop and take note, you will notice that what you earn is a lot less than what you are spending. Unfortunately, this is also unsustainable. You are getting more and more into debt.

It is obvious, but the first thing you should consider is your total income after tax. This is what you have to live on each month. You must know that figure because you can not go over it.

After you get to know your magic number, the next step is to be aware of your actual spending habits. You will have to pour over your bank and credit card statements for the past months to understand them.

Make a list of each item/service you spent your money with. You will then be able to tell where your money is going. This will bring you essential awareness. You are now aware of your true spending habits.

From that list, you will be able to see if there is anything you can eliminate, lower your expenditure on, or actually find a cheaper alternative.

Your goal is, after adding everything up, to be below your total disposable income.

Maybe it is time you look at the lifestyle you are having. If you can't afford it on your disposable income and use credit to fund it, you live beyond your means. You will have to make adjustments. Uncontrolled debt can quickly spiral you into bankruptcy.

A good result would be to spend less than you make, and an excellent result is to spend way less than you earn. This is the single most important financial habit to develop. It is also the hardest.

How do you spend less? By understanding what causes you to spend in the first place. Your spending triggers. Once you identify them, you can remove, adjust or change them.

Your lifestyle has to match your monthly income. If it ends up becoming more significant than your budget, then you could end up in worse shape indeed.

That is why having a budget is paramount. That is the money you have to spend, not more, not less. You need to fit your life around it.

Buy things intentionally; that means things you really need and not things you want. Consider your purchases carefully and delay your spending for a few days to ensure it is indispensable and worthwhile.

Living within your means will equate to living on debit and not credit. Only spend what you have because if you do spend what you do not, you will still need to pay it back, and with interest. Is it gratifying to buy an item you do not need and know you will be paying it back for a long time?

It is time to look at your finances and make a plan on how to pay the credit card balances, and the easiest way will be for you not to increase your balance anymore.

People who shop with plastic spend more than people who shop with cash. When you are shopping with cash, you can't spend more than what you have in your wallet.

You will need to be disciplined and start saving for the things you need. Remember, spend what you have got and do not live on credit. Save up for big purchases. Instead of buying something as soon as you want them, anticipate your needs, save up for them.

If you would like more money, nothing stops you from progressing in your career, finding a better job, retraining, or even finding a second job or a second income.

You need to move away from living your life for shopping and instead of finding a different meaning. Living through new and exciting experiences, spend time with the people you care about. The meaningful experiences do not have to be attached to a dollar bill.

It is easier than you think to spend more than you earn. Dipping into savings, borrowing from others, and using credit are ways you can spend more money than you bring in.

There are many reasons why you overspent. It could be because you aren't aware of your true spending habits and because you are guessing your income, expenses, debt payments, and spending incorrectly.

People don't realize how expensive consumer debt can be. If you pay a 15% credit card rate and pay the minimum each month, your credit card debt will double in five years! And if you pay a 20% interest rate, expect a doubling of debt in only 3.5 years.

Many people fund their lifestyles with debt and continue to dig deeper with no end in sight.

The single most important habit to develop is to spend less than you make. It is also the hardest.

See below some ways you can keep your spending in check:

- **Understand your spending triggers**. To know how to stop spending money has to do with identifying the triggers that cause you to spend. If you remove the triggers, you will remove the temptation and opportunity to overspend.

- **Lifestyle.** If your budget is smaller than the lifestyle you live, you could end up in worse shape. To start living within your means is to create a budget and stick to it.

- **Track your spending**. Small purchases can really add up. Tracking your expenses is the key to successfully budgeting. When you are aware of where your money is going, you will be making smarter spending choices and identifying areas you can cut back in.

  - **Delay your spending**. Wait on your decisions for a few days. This may lessen the impact of any spending trigger. Delaying can give you time to think about whether something is necessary or worthwhile.

  - **Plan a budget**. A budget is an excellent way to stay on top of your spending. If you need help putting a budget together, you may want to use a budget planner.

  - **Stop using credit cards**. With a credit card, it is easy to justify overspending. Plastic makes us feel detached from our money.

  - **Save up for big purchases**. Instead of buying things as soon as you want them, anticipate your needs and save up for them. Anticipating future upgrades and expenses is also a powerful way to protect yourself from emergency spending.

- **Find ways to increase your income**. You could be applying for a promotion, find a side hustle, or even start a part-time job.

- **Distinguish between your wants and your needs**. What you want is not necessarily what you need, and therefore it is not essential.

- **Understand what brings meaning to your life**. Move away from spending money, shopping and instead explore experiences with the people you care about. These special moments are worth a lot more than the latest gadget.

If you do not have a fixed income, it can be an issue to manage cash flow. Try finding your income baseline, which is the average of your income or your worst monthly income. You can work with that number to find what is your disposable income.

Going overdraft

Going overdraft is not something that should be happening on a monthly basis to you. If it is, then you are definitely spending more than you make. Adjusting your current lifestyle needs to happen.

It is true that an overdraft can be useful; it can also become an expensive problem if you start relying on it and don't pay it back.

Ideally, you should really never have to go overdraft. This is because you would have an emergency fund for unexpected expenses. If you are prepared, there are really very few opportunities to be caught out short that you have to dig into your overdraft.

Your bank may offer you an opportunity to have an arranged overdraft. That might be a nice buffer to have, but make no mistake, the minute you use that, you are getting into debt.

This does not equate to you dipping into your savings or your emergency fund, as these contain money you have. An overdraft is borrowing money you do not have. And as such, you will have to pay it back.

On your credit report, an overdraft will appear as a debt. If you do not use it, it will show as a zero balance. If you are using it, the amount you owe will show on your credit report.

When you use your overdraft occasionally and pay it all at the end of the month, your usage might not appear.

When you go beyond your overdraft limit, it will damage your credit rating. A lender will think you may be struggling financially.

When you have an agreed overdraft and take out more than the agreed limit, the bank may reduce or stop it.

If you go overdrawn and don't agree with this with the bank first, it is called an unauthorized overdraft and can affect your credit rating, making it harder for you to get a loan in the future.

When you have savings as well as an overdraft, it will be cheaper, in the long run, to use your savings to pay it off. Remember, overdrafts are debt, and to improve your financial outcome, debt is something you must get rid of.

You can avoid going overdrawn by having a budget and being aware of everything you pay out of your bank account, and always check your bank statements regularly. Look at all your direct debits and standing orders. Do you know what they are all for?

Check the cash withdrawals or card payments you make during the month. Itemize your spending.

As soon as you reduce your overdraft debt and get to a milestone marker, see if your bank will reduce your limit. Once the overdraft is repaid, why not lose it completely? Remove the temptation will take away the opportunity and you will have to learn how to live with what you earn.

Impulse buying

If you have not planned to buy an item and you find yourself coming out of a store or online having just done so, then this is impulse buying.

Something triggered you to buy that item. It could have been a nicely put advertisement, or you simply just liked the look of what you saw. It is all about emotions and feelings rather than logic and planning.

Most impulse buying is emotional. It is usually the result of some form of emotional distress. It could happen due to issues around self-esteem, anxiety, sadness, or even boredom.

When you are sad, anxious, stressed, and you want to go shopping, try to think about doing something else. You could go for a walk, listen to music, or call a friend. Taking care of yourself in ways that don't involve money will keep you from making those impulse purchases to self-soothe.

While there is nothing wrong with that when occasionally done and as a treat, if you do that on a regular basis, then it will be easy to reach for credit or to go overdraft as you are not planning your expenses.

Once you identify the culprit, stay well away from it and try to minimize your exposure to it in order to eliminate any impulse buying in the future.

Your purchases should be intentional. By that, it means you should only buy something you absolutely need and only after ensuring you are getting the best price.

Spur-on-the-moment purchases may give you some happiness at first but have no long-term value and are unnecessary.

When you see something you like but were not considering buying it, take a moment. Do not go ahead with the purchase right and then. Let the urge cool down for a couple of days, and then revisit it and think if the item is really needed.

Another way of you determining that is to consider how long it will take you in terms of working hours to pay for it. Knowing the value comparison may make it less appealing.

When you have had a bad day, try to stay away from stores, particularly if you use shopping to make you happy. You will be more likely to overspend in an emotional state. To relieve your daily stress, prioritize activities that get you away from shopping centers.

When out shopping, stick to a list of what you need. It is not on your list; you should not buy it.

Have a clean budget and review it every month. Creating a budget, you will stick to will help holding you accountable when you have the urge to shop.

Not setting money aside

Your aim every month is to spend a lot less than you earn. That way, you will have money left every month, and that creates many possibilities.

Saving every month will allow you to:

- Build an emergency fund

- Grow savings for future and planned expenses
- investment opportunities
- Retirement planning

There is so much you can achieve, however without a direction; your focus can waver. That is why it is important you set your financial objectives and keep revisiting them to ensure they are up to date.

If your focus is just spending what you earn, then you will not have the ability to achieve anything. A change in mindset is necessary.

The focus should be on spending less and putting money aside every month.

How important saving money is cannot be understated. It is one of the best financial habits you can adopt.

To build any kind of wealth, you are going to need to utilize the power of compound interest. If you spend all your money and never learn to save, you will miss out on this opportunity.

You can use automatic savings plan. That way, every month, a certain percentage of your earnings will go to the savings account. Do not wait until the end of the month to see if there is any money left to save; instead, transfer the money as soon as you get paid and live on the rest.

Saving will make sense, providing you do not have any more debts; otherwise, getting rid of high-interest debt makes sense before you are in too deep.

When you are ready to start, start small, then slowly increase the automated savings. When you have less money to work with, you simply learn how to make it work.

After paying the bills and living expenses, if you think your budget is too tight to be able to save anything at all, you can try to get some free cash by cutting on your living expenses:

- Changing your television service. Cancel your cable or satellite TV and switch to a cheaper alternative.

- Look at your food bill. Stop or cut back on eating out. When grocery shopping, always use a list and search for good prices.

- Switch to cash for your daily expenses. It can help you cut back on your spending. Using cash places a harder limit on your spending and helps you become more aware of your choices.

- Stop buying lunch out; instead, bring something from home to drink and eat.

Find ways to reduce your expenses, and whatever money you manage to save, put it aside. By doing that every month, you are starting to take the steps for a better financial future.

Knowing what you are saving for and how long it will take to get there is essential to becoming a smart saver. Having a timeframe helps you focus on how much you can afford to put away and how often to hit your target.

You do not have a financial plan

When it comes to financial planning, some people simply don't do it. It is clear that financial planning is the best way to make the most out of our hard-earned money.

Think of a financial plan as the steps you take to go on a vacation. You do not just go to the airport without a ticket, hotel booking, and a visa.

A financial plan is very similar. You need to know your destination in order to take steps to get there.

To reach your financial goals easily, you need to have a plan. Otherwise, you will not have an idea which goal to work on next. You will not have a focus, a direction, and therefore it will be a lot easier for you to get distracted.

An important part of a financial plan is a budget, as we have seen before. Without a budget, a plan is not going to happen by magic.

There is a general misconception of what financial planning is. Some people think planning is only for the wealthy or something you do a couple of years out from retirement. That is actually backward. Planning needs to begin in your 20s and 30s because the decision you make at that time can have the most impact on your financial future.

To prepare for the big events in your life, you will need a financial plan. The first step is creating a plan. Create a budget and break down your goals into small pieces so that you can reach them.

Coming with a financial plan is actually quite emotional, and it can be scary at times but what happens when people don't have a plan in place is far scarier.

Your goals must be realistic. There is nothing more frustrating than setting an unrealistic and unachievable objective. You are setting yourself for failure.

To get the confidence and knowledge you need to achieve larger goals that will take more time; setting short-term financial goals can help.

Life changes, and so do your priorities, so it is important to review your plan frequently and make adjustments, especially when your circumstances change.

If you have an outside expert look at your financial picture, it might reveal opportunities to make or save money. You don't necessarily need to hire someone to create a plan for you, but a lot of people do that to save themselves time and energy.

You don't shop around

When you realize you need something new, it can be hard to take the time to shop around. You may have just a short amount of time, or you might not know where to start and that already makes the whole concept of shopping around not so exciting.

It might take some effort on your part, but if you could buy something cheaper, isn't the effort worth it? After all, you could be using the saved cash for something else.

Comparing prices is essential before making a purchase because it helps consumers find a great deal on the same item. When making a purchase, you should always be able to answer 'what is the best price I can get?'.

Comparing costs across different platforms will help you save some money. There are several websites and apps dedicated to pricing tracking and comparison. To make absolutely sure you are getting the best deal, use a few different apps and extensions.

You can save money by buying in large quantities. It can be a good idea to stock up on items you need when they are on sale. Be sure you can use up what you buy.

Do not be afraid to consider generic or store brands. They are normally good products, and you are not going to pay for the name brand.

A good way to gather ideas where to start is to ask around your friends and family and find out what people are doing to find the best prices. You might find a good website, app, or store you did not know anything about.

By shopping around and reducing your costs, you are going to make your money last longer and could be allocating the saved cash to other projects.

So there are plenty of advantages to shop smarter.

You live above your means

Living beyond your means is common in our consumer and debt-heavy society. It is almost expected, but it can put us in tricky financial situations and consumer debt.

Living above one's means is like making enough money to buy a one-bedroom flat but buying a 5-bedroom detached house. You are living a lifestyle financed by credit which would normally be completely out of your reach.

The issue with that is obvious. You keep getting more and more into debt to finance a life that is not really yours to have, at least not at this moment.

Choosing to live a life on debt is not a strong foundation for a stable future. It is like a house of cards. One day it will crumble, and you will have nothing to show for it.

Some people choose a life like that due to the expectations of the people they know. One of the worst possible ways to live your life is by comparing yourself to other people. You should live your own life and not someone else's.

Ambition is good as it pushes you to grow. If you are not happy with what you can achieve at this stage, there is nothing wrong with building a strong foundation to have a more successful life.

As long as you realize the key to your happiness is not on owning things but in living experiences with the people you love. At the end of the day, this is what you are going to take with you when you die, the experiences, not the things you own.

So you see, to live within your means, you will have to have a complete shift in your mindset and current values. Only once this is done will you understand the life you could be living now.

You can tell you are living above your means if you have more than enough income for the basics, but you indulge in eating out, vacations, and overspending on clothes and cars—all at the expense of future needs.

All these things you are now buying with credit will be paid back and with interest, robbing you of a better and more stable financial future.

If all you are currently doing is paying your debts and interest, that means you are not taking steps to safeguard and invest in your future. You are always chasing how to pay for things you already bought or experienced. You are living now but your finances are still attached to the past.

You are not covered if suddenly something goes wrong, as you don't have an emergency fund. You will have to go deeper into debt in order to sort out any emergency expenses that appear.

One of the areas you could be overspending is your housing costs. Do not let your mortgage or rent be more than 28% of your income before taxes. If you find your housing costs are too high, you might consider downsizing or finding a way to increase your income.
You drive a car you cannot afford. Leasing or buying a car comes at a cost, which is in interest, the ongoing depreciating value of the car, and maintenance expenses. If you are financing a car, spend no more than 10% of your income. You should also consider buying a used versus a new car as you can save a ton of money this way.

The retirement plan is not what it should be. You live for now. If you don't save anything for the future, you are bound to find yourself in trouble later. You can't work forever. It is best to let compound interest help you out by giving cash time to grow.

To keep on track is to have and keep a budget. Ensure you track all of your expenses and ideally look into ways to decrease all your expenditures, as this is a way to have some more extra cash each month.

Aim to underspend your paycheck every month. That way, you can then concentrate on paying your debts, saving money for future purchases, investing, and having a retirement plan.

Living paycheck to paycheck interferes with your ability to build wealth because your assets are continuously shrinking while your liabilities are continuously growing.

When you are not completely satisfied with your disposable income, it is a perfect opportunity to evaluate your career, retrain or even just find a side job to generate more income.

To get your finances in order, start paying off debts, as this has the potential to be one of the best ways to get money back in your life for good.

Analyze how you are spending. Are you paying for services that you could be doing yourself?

Living within your means is an absolutely necessary step in your quest for financial success.

Chapter 4

You are not sticking to a budget

You have done the homework and know how much you have got to spend after taxes and expenses. It is not easy, though, to stick to it.

You might be tempted to buy things you see and like, and you are not really too worried if you have to use credit.

You have an idea when you have to pay your bills, but as you are not keeping an accurate track, you might end up paying your bill late or even finding yourself having to use the overdraft.

When you have lived for so long being able to do everything you wanted, it is now hard to stick to living within your means. It is hard, it is not fun, and you are finding it hard.

Keeping a budget is not easy, but it helps you reach your goals. It is not always pleasant to deny yourself things you want, but your goal should not be short-term satisfaction but actually long-term growth.

It is important at this stage to stick to your budget and continue to record ALL your expenses with no exception. It is also important to be creative and cut your expenses as much as possible.

You might be denying yourself certain things at this stage, but once you are in better financial shape, you will be able to do more. That is if you still want to do it. You might find that your priorities will shift and what you want now is not necessarily what you will want then.

At the moment, try to sleep on big purchases. If you do not need it, take a week to think about it. Weight the benefit to make sure it is adding value to your life.

You need to know how to live with what you have and never spend more than that. It can be a vicious cycle of getting into debt. You end up spending more on interest overall.

Do not be tempted to spend your credit limit on your credit card. Actually, now it is a good opportunity to analyze if you could actually decrease your credit limit. It is easy to rack up on credit cards with high limits but hard to pay down. Keep a lower credit limit and pay it off more frequently.

Try to think minimal. There is a value to minimalism from a financial perspective as well. To get you started with it, identify your needs and wants. Stick with the necessities. Cut back on the clutter.

Your day-to-day does not need to be filled by shopping all the time. Find a hobby or something you enjoy doing. To make this even more special, share with someone you love who might also have the same interest.

You never know; you might even be able to turn your hobby into an extra income.

Plan your meals, your grocery shopping so that you do not spend a fortune when you go to the supermarket. Any money not spent is money you have in your pocket.

You need to start to understand the value of things. Understand how long it takes you to make that kind of money. Connect your spending to your work. Rarely when spending money do people connect it to the labor that went into generating it.

Do not get rid of your receipts, as you will need them to record all your purchases.

In order for your budget to work, set a realistic one. Be sure to consider your majority monthly costs - rent, bills, online monthly subscription fees, student loan payments. If needed, adjust and keep it up to date. You need to be realistic and only reduce or give up on what you can afford.

You need to create goals. It will give you something to work for, so you can see when you have succeeded.

You are not paying off your credit card in full each month

If you pay your credit card balance in full each month, it can help with your credit scores. This is because by paying it back every month, you are only utilizing a small amount of your credit limit, which shows a good financial situation.

Every time you spend money on your credit card, you should only spend what you can afford to pay back every month. Leaving a balance will just cost you money in the form of interest. If you keep carrying a high balance, this will have a negative impact on your score because it will increase your credit utilization ratio.

Your credit utilization ratio shows how much of your available credit you are utilizing, and it is a factor in your credit scores.

Try to stay under 30% utilization overall. When you exceed that percentage, credit scores decrease much more rapidly.

If you carry balances, it means you are going to pay interest on your purchases, so what you bought will end up costing you more than need be.

Making minimum payments each month means you are paying interest on the remaining balance that carries over to the next billing period. Most credit cards charge compounding interest.

This means it will take years, if not decades, to pay your debt back, and that is if you stop spending on it now.

If you have a large debt on your credit card, there are some ways you can pay this back:

- Use the debt avalanche method, as this can help you save money on interest. After making the minimum payment on all your credit cards, put some extra money on the card with the highest APR. Once you paid off, move to the card with the next highest APR, and so on.

- Use the snowball method. You pay towards the credit card with the lowest balance while continuing to make the minimum payment on the rest of the cards. When the card has been paid off, concentrate on the card with the next lowest balance. In the long run, you will pay more in interest with the snowball method, but you will see progress in paying off cards sooner.

- You can consider looking into debt consolidation if you have a good credit score. You can consolidate debt by getting a balance transfer card that comes with a 0% APR for a set period. You pay no interest on the balance you have transferred during this period. You will pay less in interest, and it will help you lower the amount you owe.

- You can take out a debt consolidation loan with a lower interest rate than your credit cards have. That way, you can combine multiple balances into one loan with fixed monthly payments to save on interest.

Before choosing a strategy, check your credit score. A good credit score is required for balance transfer credit cards.

It is also important that you are paying on time, so setting up a direct debit for your credit card payments will ensure you never forget to pay.

Paying off your bill in full each month, you won't pay interest on what you have borrowed. If you make cash withdrawals, interest is charged on a daily basis from the day you take your cash. It is therefore prohibitively expensive to use your credit card on an ATM.

When going on vacation, bear in mind that deposits and pre-authorizations might reduce your credit limit. There are several businesses like hotels or car rental firms that might use your credit card to take pre-authorization.

It can take a few days until your credit limit is back to normal, even after they remove the hold.

Making late payments

Your credit score reflects how reliable you are with credit, and it affects your ability to borrow money. On-time payments are the biggest factor affecting your credit score, so missing a payment can sting.

Some companies take late payments into account when calculating your score. Overdue payments can suggest you are struggling to manage your finances.

If a late payment is recorded on your report, it will stay there for six years. Its impact on your score will reduce as the records ages. Lenders usually pay more attention to your most recent credit history.

If you can't help missing a payment, you should contact the company as soon as possible. Explain your situation, as they may be able to agree a temporary solution with you.

Companies often charge penalty fees and interest on overdue payments. Some companies will give you a grace period.

Find out how long it will take for your payment to reach your lender, as some payment methods take more than a day tor process.

Male the payment. If this was a short-term issue, make sure that you pay it back immediately.

If you are less than 30 days late, you probably were charged a late payment fee and perhaps a higher APR, but your credit won't suffer as long as you pay before the 30-day mark.

If you are more than 30 days late bring your account current as soon as possible. Thirty days late is bad, but it is not as bad as sixty. The sooner you can catch up, the less damage to your credit.

Set up regular payments. You may want to set up regular payments, such as direct debt, to ensure that you don't miss any more payments.

If you have missed a payment, the late payment can get reported to the credit bureaus once you are at least 30 days past the due date. Penalties or feeds could kick in even if you are one day late, but if you bring your account current before the 30-day mark, the late payment won't hurt your credit.

A single late payment will lead to a greater score drop if you had excellent and a clean credit history.

Credit reports sometimes include mistakes. If you spot incorrect information like a payment marked late when it wasn't, dispute the error to ask the credit bureau or the creditor involved to take it off your credit reports.

Spending too much on groceries

You might recognize this, you go to the supermarket to buy one thing, and when you come out you bought several extra things that you had not planned, but you thought you might need. This probably is a fairly common scenario. As a consequence, you ended up paying a lot more.

One of the factors that contribute to your shopping list is your family's lifestyle. Your schedule will likely determine your grocery budget, and your food preferences will determine your expenditure.

Before you decide to cut back, you will need to understand how much you are spending when you go grocery shopping. Tracking all your food expenses for a month is a great way to come up with an accurate grocery budget.

It is also important to determine how much food you are wasting each month.

In order to send less in the supermarket, you need to be aware that there are many marketing strategies being employed so that this happens. You might think you know where the washing powder is just to find out it has been moved, and now you need to cruise through the store to find it, and in the process, you get exposed to all the hundreds of other items being sold.

The sure way to prevent you from spending more is to prepare a shopping list in advance with only the items you need and, most importantly, to stick to only the items on your list.

If that seems too tempting, you might want to consider online shopping as you can easily type on the search area what it is you are looking for without having to look at the other items. Or you might want to create a favorite list with the items you buy most frequently.

Buying in bulk and the use of a freezer to preserve the food should be something to consider if you have a larger family. This might end up being cheaper.

Set a simple grocery budget. Having a budget for your food is a great way to keep control of your grocery spending. If you are throwing away food because it goes out of date before you have a choice to eat it, you are spending too much money on food.

In your highest spending categories, look for savings. For that, you will need to break down your grocery spending by category. After that, you can easily find out where you spend the most money. You can then target that category by reducing spending - clipping coupons or cutting back on eating those types of foods.

Look into different local grocery stores. Chances are you have got some cheaper grocery options local to you. Or you might find that a wholesale store membership saves a ton on food staples.

Downshift. It is fairly common to believe that if something costs more, it is better. There is nothing wrong with using the supermarket's own-branded food. Try to drop one category on everything you buy to see if you can tell the difference. If not, stick to the cheaper one.

You are buying everything new

When you need to purchase something, you should consider the possibility of getting something pre-owned versus getting something new. This is especially true with very expensive items, like a car.

The smell of a new car is great; however, just consider how much you are paying for the privilege as when you drive off the new car, it already has lost hundreds of pounds in value.

You can find very good deals if you buy a 1-2-year-old car which is relatively new and it comes with all the cons you want, but you won't be paying a huge tag because it won't be new anymore.

Life nowadays is very fast-paced, and there is always the urgency to upgrade items we already have. This is reinforced with ads, social media, and overall there is an expectation that if you are successful, you are going to have the latest and the best.

You don't have to follow everyone else. If the item you own is new, it works; why would you want to spend money replacing it?

Imagine the amount of savings you can do if you cut upgrading every little thing.

The secret is living a more minimalistic life where owning, shopping, buying, impressing other people is not your own priority. Your main priority could be having some spare time for yourself, pampering yourself, spending time doing things that really matter with the people you care about.

Let go of wanting things. Wanting is just an option your mind provides, not an order. Buying new things won't make you happier, and you know that.

Don't let yourself be manipulated. Understand what the purpose of an ad is. It is not to show you things that will improve your life and make you happy. It is to make you unhappy with what you have got so that you can then buy new things.

Wasting money on unnecessary things is not green and environmentally friendly. Whenever you replace something that is fine with something else, you are harming the planet for no real reason.

All you need to do to stop purchases that came about from a lack of awareness is realize how much money you have already wasted.

You are overloaded with subscription services

Nowadays, subscriptions are not about getting a newspaper, magazine, or gym every month. It can be about anything: wine, chocolate, make-up, delivery services, software, learning…the list is truly huge.

It is very easy to sign up for a lot of these and then, with time, not be able to enjoy what you are paying for. In time subscriptions services can inflict more damage to your finances than other types of online purchases as they are set up to charge you automatically. This makes them far too easy to keep in perpetuity. And if you are not in the habit of checking your statements, very easy to continue paying them for a very long time.

If you are not saving and investing enough to reach your financial goals, then these subscriptions are twice as bad. It is probably smart to figure out how much you are spending on them so you can determine whether it is too much or just the right amount.

Break out your last six months of bank statements and credit card bills, then look them over for subscriptions you have paid for. Then you can make a decision if you want to keep them or not.

Bear in mind that many of these services go up in price over time. Many subscription companies set low upfront pricing that they slowly raise over time. They are trying to make money, so they will entice you with a good initial offer, but then they need to recoup the money, and in time they will increase the prices.

Whenever possible, do not pay subscriptions. Lack of awareness is realizing how much money you have already wasted.

You are buying lunch everyday

A very easy way you can cut costs is by not buying lunch/snacks every day.

You can prepare what you want at home and then eat it at work or at school. It does not seem much what you spend daily; however, if you actually calculate it yearly, you will see you are spending hundreds on this.

A treat now and then will not break the bank, but as a good habit, you should be preparing healthy, free of additives food so that no only you are saving money, but you are also looking after your health.

You do not have to cook to make your own lunch. You can go raw and make a vegetable platter. If you prefer you could stick to meat and cheese.

Bringing your own food can give you a great excuse to go out for a walk and enjoy any green space and a bit of fresh air.

A homemade lunch is not only cheaper but also typically healthier because you can better control the portions and ingredients.

Most people like things that are easy. Packing lunches can be sort of inconvenient.

For many people, lunch is an opportunity to socialize, but you can also do that without having to reach for your wallet.

Chapter 5

*T*aking payday loans

This is actually one of the worse ways you can use to borrow money. These types of loans are expensive ways to borrow.

Payday loans are short-term loans originally designed to tide people over until payday. The borrowed money is paid into your bank account, and you repay in full (interest and charges) at the end of the month.

It is possible to borrow for longer periods and repay in installments. These loans are high cost and short-term, and often for small amounts.

Before a loan is agreed upon, many payday lenders will ask you to set up a recurring payment. This will allow them to take what you owe straight from your bank account via your debit card on a set date.

This can make it easier, but it is risky. It might not leave you enough money in your account for other bill payments. It could also take you over your overdraft limit, leading to bank charges.

When you have issues repaying a payday loan, the payday lender might tempt you with an extension known as deferral or rollover, or even a further loan.

Don't assume that you can't get a more suitable loan elsewhere - even if you have a poor credit rating.

If you are struggling to repay a loan, credit card, and other bills, you can get free, confidential advice from a debt advice service.

Think carefully about how you are going to pay the loan back before you decide to go ahead. Ideally, do no take one.

When taking out a payday loan, if you cannot repay it, don't take out another debt.

These products are aimed at people with limited access to mainstream credit. The amounts of money may be small, but the interest rates are high.

A large risk for those who fail to pay back their loans is getting trapped into a cycle of debt.

Interest is calculated as a percentage of the amount you borrow, and for payday loans, it is often charged daily. So if you take a large loan and take a long time to pay it back, you will end up paying more than the loan was worth in interest.

Legitimate lenders will always do some kind of credit check to make sure that you can repay them.

Avoid loan sharks at all costs. They are unlicensed, they often break the law, and they will use any means necessary to get their money repaid.

There is some alternative to a payday loan:

- borrow from friends or family
- cut back other costs
- sell something you own

Over eighteens can apply for a payday loan. Whether you are approved depends on your credit history and other financial information.

If your credit card is low, you are less likely to be approved.

Usually, your score won't be damaged by a payday loan as long as you repay it in full and on time. Any loan application can temporarily reduce your credit score due to the hard search and a new credit account being added to your profile.

If you aim to avoid a payday loan, then stick to a budget, and try and leave some money left over each month.

It is possible that getting a mortgage at a good rate will be harder if you have recently had a payday loan.

If you have used payday loans and want to apply for a mortgage:

- wait at least two years after your last payday loan was settled
- go through a good broker
- a payday loan affordability complaint may help clean up your credit record

Lenders will check your credit records when you apply for a mortgage. They might do this before giving you an agreement in principle and will recheck more thoroughly before approving your actual application.

The credit checks don't show exactly who you borrowed from, but they do show the sort of borrowing - loan, overdraft, credit card.

People in a good financial position don't need to use payday loans, so using a payday loan is seen by most mortgage lenders as a big warning sign that you had financial problems.

You have a consumer mentality

As mentioned before, adopting better money habits will require a complete mindset reset. You will have to find more meaningful values in your life to replace the unhealthy ones you might still have.

Having a consumer mentality will definitely go against having great money values as a consumer mentality demands of you to consume and spend your money, and the money habits you are trying to cultivate go the complete opposite way.

Consumer mentality is the mindset many of us have. It is about owning and having material things or constantly consuming the latest.

It is usually also to do with:

- keeping up with the joneses
- instant gratification
- showing off
- addicted to spending and shopping

Your finances can be put into some serious trouble by you having an extreme consumer mentality. It is going to take work to break the consumer habit. Making an effort at all puts you ahead of the vast majority.

The way to go is the investor mentality. This is because:
- it helps you build and save money
- eliminate high-interest consumer debt
- creates more financial stability
- builds long-term wealth for the future

Spending money in moderation is okay. To help you build wealth, minimize your consumption and increase the production of assets.

Make it a priority to make changes. If you don't dedicate time to breaking the consumer mentality, it is not going to happen.

See where all your money is going. This means making a budget, keep track of money coming in and going out.

Why do you feel the need to consume? What is the trigger behind any excess consumption? Find the reasoning for your consumer mindset.

You should concentrate on what financial goals you may have.

Start reading investment books. They help you understand and learn about great financial habits.

Owning less brings great benefits to our lives: less stress, less debt, more time, more freedom. Wanting less brings even more. It allows wonderful habits to emerge: contentment, gratitude, freedom from comparison.

Become aware of the consumer-driven society in which we live. Nobody would ever say the secret to a joyful, meaningful life is to buy a lot of stuff.

Stop and reevaluate. Look at the life you have created.

Stop copying other people.

Do more of what makes you happy. Find what is true makes you happy and do more of it.

Worrying about impressing others

It is a very connected world we all live in. We can keep up to date with what other people are doing on social media, and it is very easy to compare ourselves with other people.

If someone you know posts a picture of a beautiful brand new car, it is not unnatural for you to compare it to what you drive at the moment. From there, it is only natural you start thinking about possibly upgrading your car for a newer one or, even better, buying yourself a new car too.

The same for mobile phones, clothes, appliances; the list could be endless and very exhausting.

Changing your mindset will see to that too. If you own something and it still provides you with a value, there is really no reason for you to replace the item. Why pay a lot more for something that is new and that in the end it will only be bought to impress other people? It is not really serving a purpose to you, and that is all that matters.

If you put yourself in debt to purchase something you really did not plan or need, you are unbalancing your whole financial plan and will have to postpone doing the great things you had planned. For what? At the end of the day, it is you who will be left paying the bill, literally.

You should stop and reflect on the ways you spend money; you will find that some things are really not connected to what other people think. A lot of what you spend does revolve around or are heavily influenced by what others think of you.

To get better control over your finance and personal success, the first step is to stop spending any money or any time impressing others.

Find ways to invest your time and energy in effective ways of impressing yourself and building a better life so that you won't have. Instead, devote your time and energy to effective ways of impressing yourself so that you do not need to spend a lot of money.

Ensure that you concentrate every day on becoming the person you want to be and not pretending to be what you think other people will be impressed by.

A lot of financial problems can be sorted by focusing your attention on being the best you can be and stop spending time on things that are largely influenced by impressing others.

Living trying to impress people all the time is going to affect how you feel. When you gain the approval of others, it is going to be for what you are doing and not for who you are.

When you feel the need to always impress others in order to be accepted, it is probably because you feel that other people won't accept you for who you are. You are likely to feel as though you are not enough and that in order to be enough, you need to constantly impress others.

Relying on credit to pay bills

You should be paying your bills with your monthly income and not with credit. Using credit to pay expenses will end up costing you a lot of money in the long run.

If that is the case now, you have got to look at your budget, expenses and make some drastic cuts so that you will be able to use your monthly income to pay the bills and only use credit occasionally.

Paying by credit anything and everything is pretty much a way of life for many people. Credit in itself is not a bad thing. Always relying on it to pay for living costs is not something you can do over the long term.

Credit lets you make purchases sooner rather than later. You are essentially putting off paying until another day. However, pay you will eventually, and with all that added interest.

You are being charged interest on these purchases, and this is often quite high.

By the time you have entered year two, three, or even four, you have paid hundreds or thousands in interest alone.

If you are forced to rely on credit cards to pay your bills, and you rack up a high enough balance to exceed the 30% credit utilization, your credit score can start to suffer. It will make it more difficult for you to borrow money the next time you need to.

By understanding your budget, you will have a better idea of how much money you can save each month towards the big one-off expenses.

There is a catch with paying the minimum on credit cards. Minimum payments only clear a small amount of your balance. The payment is mainly going towards interest and charges on the balance you owe.

Emergencies happen to everyone. When you have one, you might have no choice but to put it on your credit card. However, if you have already got a high credit balance, this extra cost may make your situation worse.

When having an emergency fund to fall back on, you are less likely to rely on credit if something bad happens.

If you use your credit cards a lot, you should be mindful of your credit utilization rate. The lower your utilization rate, the better it is for your credit scores.

Use debit cards. They offer an easy way to control spending and the convenience of plastic without the risks. Debit cards only let you use money that you have rather than letting you borrow money.

Don't use your credit cards for cash withdrawals. You will be charged fees and higher interest for the whole period until you pay it off.

Credit can be expensive, and if not used properly, it can become a trap.

Not taking control of your career

Successful people in their careers are the ones who have taken charge. They deny waiting and seek options themselves.

Work is an important part of our lives, so having a connection with what you do seems to be the key.

Once you found your niche, this is not it. For you to grow and become better at it, you need to keep developing yourself. Further studies, courses, and interaction with the people in your field will give you the tools to explore what else you can do and in what direction you want to head.

Do not isolate yourself. Keep up with the learning, new developments, and keep at it. That way, you are up to date with new developments and might even be able to change in a positive way things that you have been doing in a certain way.

When you care about what you do, and you continuously work at improving yourself and your knowledge, then you are actively taking control of your career. You are not just coasting by and let things happen. You are making them do.

You might want to negotiate your salary if you think you need a welcome and deserving boost. There is nothing wrong with it. It is actually one of the best ways to boost your income. Don't be shy, be brave!

Identify your goals and set them which you want to accomplish. Just like having a financial plan, it is important to have a career one too. Having a direction, a clear go will help you get where you want to be.

Are you purposedly postponing asking what you deserve? Take advantage of all opportunities.

Network with everyone, with professionals at work, at networking events, and professional organizations. They are an excellent way to meet contacts who may help you find your next job or simply be a good resource when needed.

Seek a guide that has experience in the same path as yours. The mentor will guide through the process and advise. A mentor is someone who can give sincere and truthful feedback and who you can trust.

It is very easy to identify what you are not happy with in terms of your career but a lot harder to be clear on what is important to you, and why. You need to make the time so that you can reflect on your career to date and the decisions you have made.

You need to have an idea of what you want. Imagine yourself in the future and imagine that you are totally satisfied with your career.

How does your strength align with the goals of your role, your organization, and your industry?

It is not only things that warrant marketing, but your own brand needs it too. You need to understand the art of self-marketing and develop your personal brand making sure you communicate why you do well, how you make a difference, and the kinds of challenges and projects you would like to take on.

Become an expert in an area of importance to your company can lead to promotions and other career opportunities. Know the company and industry you work for. Read the newspaper or company's newsletters.

For you to be considered for a promotion or career progression, you will need to stand from the crowd.

Changes are scary, but they can be good too. Be open to them. See them as challenges you need to overcome and an opportunity.

If you have been working hard and feel demotivated and bad, you can take charge of your life. It is not worth staying in a job you are miserable in.

This job is the path through which you are going to make a successful career. If you hate it, you will not be able to touch success.

Not educating yourself about personal finance

One of the things that are hard to understand is that in most formal education systems today, one very important aspect of life is just not covered at all. Very little is taught about money. Its aspects, how to generate it, how to manage and invest it, and its place in society.

Due to this lack of finance teaching, motivated individuals have to take the initiative to educate themselves. This can be done by reading books, internet content, short courses, or by the advice of mentors.

Even though you are not a businessman or an entrepreneur, you should still understand how finance works.

You have to take responsibility for your life as an adult, and that does include your finances. It is OK to speak to experts in the area, but you will need to understand what people are actually talking about.

It is not a good idea to let someone else be in charge of your finances. At the end of the day, with an informed opinion, you should be the one deciding what to do with your money,

Suppose you are wondering how you can understand about something you were not really taught before or educated in previously. The answer is, in the same way, you learned so much in your life. By curiosity, interest, and dedication.

You can start reading about finance through books, go to courses and talk to the people who know more than you do. If you immerse yourself in it, you will learn a whole lot more than what you know now.

It will take time and effort on your part, but it surely is for a good cause, your financial freedom.

Understanding financial basics allow you and others to make smarter money choices and be able to be self-sufficient in financial decisions.

Reaching financial literacy means you have an understanding in a few core areas:

- Budgeting and setting financial goals
- Paying bills and saving money
- Basics of loans

- credit cards and credit scores
- how investing works

Money does not control you anymore; now, you hold the reins your attitude towards finance changes.

When you have financial education, you start to really understand how debt works, interest rates, and how to avoid debt disasters.

Financial literacy can really impact your knowledge about identity fraud in the finance space.

Income doesn't just mean your wages. Taxable income also includes interest from bank accounts, profit from selling any goods or services, and even some state benefits.

To make more money, you need to learn how to invest, and this can result in you having a really solid source of money on your side.

Do not worry about making more money; focus your energy on making good decisions with the money you have now.

Your emotions should not direct your financial decisions. Otherwise, you will be making irrational choices that can have disastrous consequences.

When becoming financially literate, it is important to create a money mindset and find a healthy process that truly works for you.

A new great habit is becoming financially savvy.

Not spending wisely

According to some people, financial issues occur because they do not bring in enough money. For others, the problem comes from not spending wisely the money you have got.

In an unstable economic climate like now, many people are becoming more aware of their spending habits. People who spent freely and paid little attention to personal debt before are now paying more attention to how they feel when they make decisions that affect their finances.

Far too many purchases are impulse decisions. Before you buy, think about how that purchase will affect your future. Have you got money to pay for it now? Or are you going to buy it on credit and spend the next months/years paying for it and adding more to your debt?

Nowadays, obtaining and maintaining a certain image is the goal, but keeping up with the Joneses can be a very expensive endeavor. Consider buying the things that you yourself enjoy and that bring a purpose to your life.

If you want to track your finances properly, you can begin by looking at the habits that may be recking with your budget.

Spending money wisely basically means getting the most for your money in line with what matters to you.

Avoid relying on credit for unexpected expenses. Your top priority should be building up your emergency savings.

Money will give you an urge to spend on things that really don't matter. If you don't have to spend on something, just don't.

Know when to spend more for quality. If you need to buy something, it makes sense you buy it fewer times and that it lasts longer. Quality items do not always equate to expensive price tags. Sometimes all you are paying for is a name.

Break free of expensive habits. Compulsive habits such as smoking, drinking, or gambling can easily consume any money you save. It is easier said than done as most of these are addictions, but if you really recognize they are not adding any benefit to your life, you are already taking the first step to freedom,

Chapter 6

Good money habits

If you want to be better at managing your money, you will have to adopt some good money habits to ensure you are doing your best to grow your money and reduce/eliminate debt.

The key to reaching your money goals is building a collection of smaller everyday habits. Building good money habits can increase wealth and set you up for financial success.

It is vital to stop bad money habits as soon as possible. Money is important. When you have the money, you will not be destitute. You are not dependent on being employed and living paycheck to paycheck.

Money gives you the possibility of some control over your life, freedom to find and take your own path, having fewer constraints on your choices. It will not be a constant struggle just to survive.

With the money, you can live life to the fullest, enjoy adventures, make the most of the years you have got.

Get on a budget

Consider this as one of the most important things you could do. Create your budget and stick to it. Divide your financial goals into short, medium, and long-range categories to make sure you are planning for your present and your future.

You need a way of determining where your money is going each month. Try to find a way to track your finances in a way that works for you.

Note your net income. You need to start with a figure: the amount of money you have coming in. Remember to subtract your deductions. The final take-home pay is called net income, and that is the number you should use when creating a budget.

You might be able to generate more income independent of your job. Have you got a hobby or a special talent? You might be able to put them to use and increase your income. An extra source of income can be extremely helpful if you ever lose your job.

One of the advantages of a budget is that it allows you to track your spending. You can begin by listing all your fixed expenses. These are regular monthly bills. It is unlikely you will be able to cut back on these.

An area where you may find opportunities to cut back is your variable expenses. Remember, your goal is not to spend all your money but to actually spend as little as possible. You can examine your variable expenses and make serious savings on them.

A budget on its own is not going to work miracles. You must have a direction, a goal. Set your goals. You have to be clear on all the financial goals you want to accomplish in the short and- long term. Aim to achieve the short-term goals in no longer than a year .

A budget is an always evolving number. Keep checking in. It is a wise move to review your budget on a regular basis to be sure you are staying on track.

You have to understand the concept of assets and liabilities. What you own are your assets, and the debts or liabilities you have determined your net worth. As mentioned before, you should aim to keep your liabilities as low as possible.

When was the last time you checked your credit report? You need to do it regularly to ensure it matches your current situation, and it will also show you a snapshot of your credit health. It contains information about the status of your credit accounts and your bill-paying history. A good score is critical to qualifying for loans at the best possible rates.

In the short term, you are trying to reduce and eliminate your debt. In the long-term, you will be looking at investment opportunities and thinking about your retirement.

When you open a retirement account or buy an insurance policy, you will be asked to name a beneficiary. Check your beneficiaries yearly to make sure they are still appropriate.

It is not an exciting part of life, but it happens to everyone: taxes. You have got to manage them. It is important to make sure you have enough set aside to pay your tax bill well before the annual deadline.

You want to protect yourself and what you are working so hard to build. That means at some point, you will look to get the right insurance. It is important to assess the type and amount of insurance you need.

The most important long-term goal anyone can have is saving for retirement, and that requires saving and investing most of your working life.

The 50/20/30 budget rule.

If you ever wondered what percentage of your income should be spent on expenses or the things you could buy, you could use the 50/20/30 budget rule.

Senator Elizabeth Warren popularised this rule in her book. The rule is to divide after-tax income and allocate it to spend 50% on needs, 30% on wants, and saving 20%.

This budget rule is an intuitive plan to help you reach your financial goals. You should aim to spend as follows:

- 50% corresponds to needs. Needs are those bills that you must pay and are the things necessary for survival. To cover your needs or obligations, you should not have to spend more than half of your after-tax income. If you are spending more than that, you will have to either cut down on wants or try to downsize your lifestyle.

- 30% corresponds to wants. They are all the things you spend money on but are not absolutely essential.

- 20% corresponds to savings. Ideally, a minimum of 20% of your net income should go to savings or investments. Adding money to the emergency fund in a savings account is an example.

Every household should prioritize creating an emergency fund in case of job losses, unexpected medical expenses, and other emergencies.

It is necessary not to guess or estimate what that money is. For the budget to be successful, you need to have an accurate idea of incoming and outgoings. To be 100% sure of what that figure is, you will have to go through all your statements and bills to be absolutely sure of how much you are spending.

If you have debts, it makes sense to pay off the debt that charges the highest rate of interest first.

This method is only a rule of thumb and, therefore, only a rough guideline on what you should be spending your money on.

Live below your means

Basically, that means spending less than what you earn. Living beyond your means results in debt; living below gives you the opposite - debt freedom.

You aim to have a more stable financial future. Once you have created a budget, consider tracking your spending. Recording each purchase is a great way to force yourself to think twice before buying something.

With credit cards, stay with only one or two to resist the temptation of overspending. It is also recommended to have a credit card utilization below 30 percent. This will help your credit score to remain healthy.

Certain expenses such as living expenses cannot be decreased unless you downsize your house, for example.

Other expenses you can control. Start by looking at memberships. Try to avoid them if you can, but if you cannot, ensure only the things you use the most are the ones you are paying for. Cancel all the rest.

When it comes to buying cars, you do not need to put yourself on credit just to impress other people. Do not buy new as you will lose a lot of money. Buy used and buy something you like that is also meant to be useful to your day-to-day needs.

Buy only what you need and only after shopping around for the best price.

If you are really looking to live below your means, finding a second form of income can get you there.

When you live below your means, you can achieve financial freedom. As you will be out of debt, this will enable you to save more money for unexpected expenses or events.

To start saving money immediately, it is essential to start living below your means now.

On the other hand, living above your means can be expensive in many ways. You will pay high amounts of interest on what you spend. You might think you can afford it, but that doesn't mean you can.

The money you are not spending can then go towards building your net worth.

The satisfaction of having a new object fades when the bill comes, and you experience the stress of trying to juggle your bills when you get paid.

Living above your means can create pressure for you to look for a higher-paying job but   at the expense of your quality of life.

When you live below your means, you can make more rational decisions about what career you want to carve out for yourself.

You can have the time to search for the right opportunity for you, the one where you can grow in your career on your own terms and the one that brings the quality of life you are looking for.

You have to do these three things to live below your means:

- Keep purchases reasonable
- Track your monthly expenditure
- Cut expenses as much as you can

Living below your means gives you the power to handle an unexpected car repair or medical bill. A healthy starting point is to live on at least 15% less than the amount you earn.

When you have no debt and savings, you have far more options in life.

In order to live below your means, you will have to trade the short-term pleasure for the long-term gain. Your higher priority should be on saving rather than spending.

Every amount spent should have a purpose, and every purchase requires thought and intentionality.

Many experts will tell you that to get rich; you should live below your means.

Saving 15% to 20% of your take-home income is the single most important thing you can do for your financial security.

The trick to accumulating wealth isn't just living below your means but living far below your means. To accumulate more money, you need to widen the gap between how much you earn and how much you spend.

Ideally, you should concentrate on earning more and at the same time spending less. The larger the gap is, the more money you can save and invest.

Reducing your expenses is often more manageable than earning more money.

The easiest way to stop spending money is to stop wanting more stuff in your life.

Pay off debt

If you have any debt, then the first thing you should be doing is trying to pay it off. Carrying debt can have a ripple effect across your entire financial life, including your credit scores.

There are two types of debt:

- **Revolving debt**. It comes from credit cards where you can carry, or revolve, a balance from month to month. The interest rates are subject to change.
- **Installment debt**. It comes from mortgages, car loans, and personal loans. The amount of money your borrow, the interest rate, and the size of your monthly payments are fixed at the start.

With both types of debt, you must make payments on time. If you miss a payment, your lender could report it to the credit bureaus, and this can stay on your credit reports for seven years.

The way each type of debt affects your credit is quite different. With installment debt, having a high balance doesn't have a big impact on your credit.

With revolving debt, if you carry high balances compared to your credit limits on your credit cards month to month, it will likely have a negative effect on your credit scores.

The percentage of available credit you are using carries significant weight in calculating your credit scores. To maintain good credit, you should keep balances low on your credit cards and ideally pay off the full statement balances each month.

Revolving debt can be so overwhelming because credit card interest rates are typically really high. If you are just making the minimum payment each month, it will take a long time to pay off your balance.

The strategy for having only one debt is simple: make the biggest monthly debt payment you can handle. Repeat until it is all gone.

If you have multiple accounts to manage, it is recommended to use the debt avalanche method since it is the best way to pay off multiple credit cards when you want to reduce the amount of interest you pay.

Avalanche method. You will pay off your account in order from the highest interest rate to the lowest.

- you pay the minimum on all your accounts
- pay as much as possible towards the account with the highest interest rate

When you pay off an account, you will free up more money each month to put towards the next debt.

This method will help you pay less in interest and will get you out of debt more quickly. It will take you longer to see progress than with the debt snowball.

Snowball method. You will pay off your debt in order from the smallest balance to the largest.

- Pay the minimum on all your accounts
- Pay as much as possible towards the account with the smallest balance

This method is loved by many people because it includes a series of small successes at the beginning. There is also the potential to improve your credit scores quickly, as you lower your credit utilization on individual credit cards sooner and reduce your number of accounts with outstanding balances.

If you have several small debts to pay this method can be the one for you. When facing several debts, this method lets you see progress as quickly as possible.

The snowball method's big downside is you will typically end up paying more over time compared to the avalanche method.

Balance transfers. When you can transfer the balance from an account with a high interest rate to a card with a lower one, you will spend less on interest over time. You are using a card to pay off another.

Balance transfers can work well with the avalanche method. When you transfer, it buys you time to focus on the next-highest interest account.

It is possible you will have to pay a balance transfer fee, so be sure to run the number and read the fine print upfront.

Personal loan. Using a personal loan to pay off credit card debt can be a smart strategy.

- Compare different loan providers to find out the rates you are likely to get and the fees involved. If you get a lower rate than you are paying now, a consolidation loan could be a good idea.

Consolidation of credit card debt with a personal loan may help your credit scores. You can significantly boost your credit when paying off your credit card debt with an installment loan.

A personal loan can mitigate overload. To make managing your debts easier, you can use a personal loan to reduce the number of payments you need to make each month.

Credit card interest rates are often higher than personal loan interest rates.

Once you pay off credit cards, do no close them but keep them open to help your credit utilization.

One thing you can do to help out afterwards is to not spend any more money on your paid-off credit cards.

Debt settlement. If you can afford to make large, one-time settlement payments to your creditors, this strategy usually works best.

The creditor accepts a partial payment to satisfy your credit card debt rather than have the full balance.

Bankruptcy. Bankruptcy can offer a fresh start. Because bankruptcy can devastate your credit, you should only use it as a last resort.

Tips on how to keep you on track:

1. Know your budget. Making the most of money coming in and going out will help you stay focused.

2. Lower your bills. By cutting what you are paying towards bills every month, you will have more cash to put toward your debt payoff.

3. Make more money. Pick up a hustle or two and increase your earning power.

4. Consider consolidation. If you want to be putting more money towards your balance, debt consolidation with a personal loan or a credit card can lower your interest rate.

5. Debt relief. If you are not making any progress on your debts, you might want to get some help.

Automate your finances

To ensure your payments are happening on time and that you are automatically saving money every month, you could automate your finances.

Great idea if you have a steady flow of income every month but not so great if that is not the case as if the money leaves your account and you have no money in, then you could be going overdrawn.

Direct deposit.

Automate how you get paid. Direct deposit has become the norm for businesses and payroll companies.

Simplify your bills.

Most bills would be around the same time of the month. It helps to get all your bills around payday.

Set up bills on autopay

In most cases, you can set your bills on auto-pay through your own bank.

Late bill payments can destroy your credit card and put you into debt.

Automating your finances can help you achieve specific goals by creating positive long- term habits while fighting the temptation to deviate from your financial plans.

The automation system can also bite you. To prevent this, you must have money in your account to help protect you against overdrafts or other expenses that can result from a mismatch in the timing of automatic bill payments and your paycheck.

On the days your paycheck hits your checking account, immediately direct a portion towards your emergency fund and retirement savings.

It is essential for you to be contributing something towards your emergency fund and retirement.

Automate your contributions to your investment accounts.

This process, known as dollar-cost averaging, also allows you to diversify your purchase price by making regular investment purchases over time.

Find a way to automatically increase your savings over time. Many online investment platforms will allow you to increase your recurring contributions on an annual basis.

You will be setting up your bill payments and savings accounts to be paid every month automatically.

Credit monitoring

Being curious and monitoring your credit rating is recommended as this can affect the rates you pay and, consequently, the amount you owe in interest.

There are some services that will not only help you track your credit, but they will give you suggestions on how to improve it.

Automate with budgeting tools

You do need to be alerted when your spending gets out of control or a rogue purchase hits your checking account.

Build your emergency fund

You should be prepared for any emergencies, extra expenses that occur without having to dig into your credit cards, savings or any investments. That is why you should build an emergency fund.

An emergency fund is an essential part of a solid financial plan.

An emergency fund is a bank account with money set aside to pay for large, unexpected expenses, such as:

- medical expenses
- home-appliance repair or replacement

- car fixes

- unemployment

Emergency funds create a financial buffer that can keep you afloat in time of need without having to rely on credit cards or high-interest loans. It can be especially important to have an emergency fund if you have debt, because it can help you avoid borrowing more.

The right amount depends on your financial circumstances, but a good rule of thumb is to have enough to cover three to six months' worth of living expenses.

Because an emergency can strike at any time, having quick access is crucial. So it shouldn't be tied up in a long-term investment fund. The account should be separate from the bank account you save daily, so you are not tempted to dip into your reserves.

A high-yield savings account is a good place for your money. The money earns interest, and you can access your cash quickly when needed.

To start with, the first step in the process is to figure out how much you spend each month. Once you know your total expenses for each month, multiply that number by three. Reaching that number will be your initial goal.

Buying a less expensive car and downgrading your cell phone service are two easy ways to come up with some cash to fund your savings plan.

The key is to add to the fund at regular intervals. Ideally, you should treat it like any other recurring bill you must pay each month.

Many market fund and high-interest savings accounts are two good places to park your emergency fund. You need safe, liquid options so that your money is accessible in times of need.

Increasing your cash flow and cutting back on expenses can make a world of difference.

Getting a side hustle is another way to boost your income. The more money you have got coming in, the more money you have available to pay existing debts and to build your emergency fund.

Set up a direct deposit that takes a portion of your pay check and automatically puts it into your emergency fund. This will help you regularly save.

Over time, increase the amount you are contributing by one percent . You might not even notice a small increase in savings. Do this regularly until you have reached your savings goal.

Emergencies may require more than a six-month cushion, so keep saving after reaching your goal.

Chapter 7

Grow your money by investing

Once you build your emergency fund, you might want to think about saving some money in order to invest. This is a way to make your money work for you.

Your financial situation is unique; therefore, the best way to invest money will depend on your personal preferences and circumstances.

When trying to become wealthy, you will need to do more than simply earn money. You will need to learn how to invest it.

Investing will allow you to have significant growth in your money over time, thanks to the power of compound returns. For you to take advantage of that, you will need to leave your money earning interest over interest. You are looking into investing over medium to long-term so that you have a shot at growing your money considerably.

Investing involves risk; however, doing nothing can cost you a lot, even considering when you lose a little on a bad investment. It is up to you if you are up to risk your money; however, you will make a lot more rather than just leaving the money standing inside a savings account as interests are so low.

For you to earn more money over time, the sooner you start saving, the more your money will earn overtime.

Know what your financial goals and timeframe are and how you feel about risk.

Decide whether you want to take a do-it-yourself or manage it for me approach.

There are many types of investments. You need to educate yourself about them to choose the best for your circumstances.

To buy most types of stocks and bonds, you will need an investment account. Some accounts offer tax advantages if you are investing for a specific purpose. Keep in mind that you may be taxed or penalized if you pull your money out early.

Mutual funds. A professionally managed investment that collects your money with other investors. The managers then will use the pooled money to buy securities for the group.

Start by investing in mutual funds or ETFs rather than stocks and bonds until you learn and feel more confident.

They are not only safer investments, but it is often far less expensive to invest this way. You will either pay just one trading commission or nothing at all.

You will save money on commissions by buying funds directly through a mutual fund company rather than a brokerage account.

Several mutual fund companies will require an initial minimum investment of between $500 and $5,000. Some will, but some will waive the account minimums if you agree to automatic monthly investments of between $50 and $100.

Bonds. It is a way of leveraging your investment against the success of other entities. It raises capital for others.

Robo-advisors. Financial advisors use algorithms to provide you with the very best advice about financial investments.

They are extremely popular at this point because they make investing accessible for everyone.

There is no investment broker, and the costs are lower as compared to traditional management firms.

Robo-advisors make investing as simple and accessible as possible. You don't need any investing experience, as they take all of the guesswork out of investing.

To learn about your goal and your risk tolerance, they ask you some questions and then will invest your money in a highly diversified low-cost portfolio of stocks and bonds. Then they use algorithms to continually rebalance your portfolio and optimize it for taxes.

Most robs-advisors require $500 or less to start investing and charge very modest fees based upon the size of your account.

They charge an annual fee equal to a small percentage of your balance. The average is about 0.25%. Bear in mind that the Robo-advisors fees are on top of the fees charged by the exchange-traded funds that robot-advisors buy to make up your portfolio.

Stocks. Take a slow approach if you are buying individual stocks. Don't put more than 10% of your portfolio in individual stocks until you get very comfortable with what you are doing.

Do not be afraid of the stock market; it really is one of the best places to grow your money. In order to do that, learn to understand how the stock market works.

Real estate. It can be a path to great earnings - even make millions.

It is a long-term investment that investors invest in for cash flow. The cash flow will also increase over time because rents will go up with inflation while your mortgage payments stay the same.

There are so many types of properties you could purchase. Knowing who you want to reach is the key.

Retirement accounts. An IRA provides certain tax advantages. How much you can contribute and when you can withdraw the money are defined by limits.

It is important to know when it is best to have a financial advisor and when it is best to opt for a different investing platform.

Developing good habits is the key to building wealth - like regularly putting money away every month. Once you save some money, you can start to invest.

High-yield savings account. They are accessible vehicles for your cash. Online banks will earn you much higher interest rates. You can typically access the money by quickly transferring it to your primary bank or even via an ATM.

It works well for risk-averse investors. Savings account are about as liquid as your money gets.

Certificates of deposit. They are issued by banks and generally offer a higher interest rate than savings accounts. They have specific maturity dates, so if you withdraw the money earlier, you will pay the penalty.

You are paid interest at regular intervals. Once it matures, you get your principal back plus any accrued interest.

Cryptocurrency. It is a kind of digital electronic-only currency that is intended to act as a medium of exchange. Bitcoin is becoming the leading digital currency and its price fluctuates a lot.

Investing in cryptocurrency is for an investor who does not mind high risk and that their investment can go to zero in exchange for the potential of much higher returns.

They are generally liquid, and you can buy and sell them at any time of day.

Trade commodities. Trading gold and silver, for example, present a rare opportunity.

The price of commodities is driven by fundamentals. As supply dips, demand increases, and prices rise.

Metals, energy, and agriculture are other types of commodities.

Venture into entrepreneurship. The act of creating a business or business while building and scaling it to generate profit. It is also about solving big problems and creating about social change or an innovative product. You build a life on your own terms. No bosses.

Get there right insurance

Insurance is meant to safeguard us should certain things happen. You need to protect your assets to ensure continuity, so choosing one or several insurances will be a necessity. Understanding all the different types will help you select the most appropriate for your circumstances.

Life insurance

A life insurance will provide the ability to cover your funeral expenses and provide for those you leave behind.

You will need to work out how much money you need to protect your dependents. This sum must take into consideration their living costs, as well as any outstanding debts.

A set amount is paid out when you die during the term and the policy will last for a set number of years.

The policy can cater for a fixed debt, such as a mortgage, or it can pay a lump sum for your dependants.

- Mortgage protection or decreasing term insurance

The policy will last for an agreed number of years which will normally match how many years you have outstanding on your mortgage payments.

Every passing year the pay-out decreases as your mortgage will decrease in time.

This policy is cheaper than level term insurance.

  - Family income benefit insurance.

This type of insurance pays out a regular income for the remaining term rather than a lump sum.

You can match your current or future take-home salary to make sure your family won't need to change their standard of living.

  - Whole-of-life insurance.

It covers you for the rest of your life so your dependants get a pay-out no matter when you die.

This type of policy is typically more expensive than those that cover a set period of time.

Contents insurance

Making sure you have the right amount of cover is essential - you do not want to pay more than you need, too little cover, and your insurance company might not payout if you need to claim.

There are three types of policies available in the market:

- Bedroom rated. The insurer works out the amount of contents cover based on the number of bedrooms you have. You do not have to work out how much insurance you need.

- Sum insured. You have to calculate the number of contents cover you need.

- Unlimited sum insured. All your contents are covered without limit so you don't have to worry about being underinsured.

What is your insurer's definition of valuables? This can vary widely. Then you need to check the single article limit. This corresponds to the most the insurer will payout in the event of a claim.

If you have an item worth more than the single article limit, you need to tell your insurer about it.

With some content policies you will be covered for the things you take out the home such as your phone or your laptop.

A standard cover might include the cost of replacing your mobile phone handset or your laptop, but you will need to check whether it covers things like music downloads on your phone or the files you have saved on your computer. Some policies include cover for digital information.

Most policies won't cover you if these items break down. And a standard contents policy won't typically cover any money you lose if someone steals your mobile phone and runs up a huge bill.

Get enough coverage to replace all your possessions. If not, you could be in for a nasty shock because your insurer might reduce the amount they payout.

You can get two different kinds of cover available, both of which have an effect on the price of your premium.

- New for old. You will get paid what it costs to replace the items.
- Indemnity cover. You will only get the current value of your possessions.

Maintain your insurance company up-to-date with your circumstances.

One curiosity is that some standard policies will not offer you cover if you have a lodger so it is very important that if you do take one, to let the insurer know about it.

Buildings insurance.

It should cover the cost of rebuilding your home if it is damaged or destroyed. It is usually compulsory if you are planning to buy your home with a mortgage.

It should also cover the cost of repairing damage to the structure of your property. The policy should cover the full cost of rebuilding your house. The market price you paid for your home is not the same as the cost of rebuilding it. Rebuilding costs are typically less than the current value of the property.

You should regularly review the amount your building insurance cover as rebuilding costs tend to rise over time.

Travel insurance.

If something goes wrong on your holiday having a travel insurance can provide you with some protection.

It is advisable to take one particularly if you are traveling independently.

A cover can protect you against:

- the cancellation or shortening of your holiday
- the case of missed or delayed transport

- medical and other emergencies
- personal injury or death
- lost, stolen, or damaged items.

It is important to think about:

- where you are traveling to
- How old you are. Travel insurance costs more if you are over sixty-five.
- How often you travel. When you travel a lot, it makes sense to buy an annual travel policy.
- The reason you will be traveling. If you practice dangerous sports, you will need to take extra cover.
- Traveling independently or as a packaged holiday. When you buy a package holiday, you have greater protection with regards to transport and accommodation if things go wrong.
- Your mode of transport. Some insurance policies will not cover cruises or budget airline flights.

Your insurance should include the following:

- cover for medical expenses and cover to get you home if you are ill abroad

- personal injury and cover for accidents or damage caused by you
- cover for lost or damaged items
- cover for lost or delayed baggage
- cover for cancellation or missed departure

Vehicle insurance

The main types of policies are:

- Third-party. This is the minimum legal requirement. It covers for damage to someone els's vehicle or property and/or injury to someone else in an accident. Repairs to your own vehicle are not included.
- Third-party, fire, and theft. In the event of fire of theft it will cover damage or loss to your own car.
- Comprehensive cover. This will include repairs to your own car. It may also cover death or injury of yourself or a family member, cover for items stolen from your car, cover for medical or legal expenses and hiring a replacement vehicle.

Policies tend to run for a year, and insurers also tend to send you a renewal notice.

Income protection insurance.

In case you can't work because of sickness or disability it will pay you a regular income until you return to paid work or you retire.

It will not pay the exact amount you were getting from your work, expect to receive around half of it.

You cannot claim this insurance straightaway. You need to wait at least four weeks.

Critical illness insurance.

If you are diagnosed with certain illnesses or disabilities it will provide you with a lump sum of money.

The illnesses covered are usually long-term and very serious conditions.

Health Insurance

The least expensive option may be participating in your

employer's insurance program. If you don't have health insurance through an employer, check with trade organisations or associations about possible group health coverage.

You might need to buy private health insurance if that is not an option for you.

Conserve your utilities

You can save significant amounts of money on your monthly utility bill by making small changes, such as turning off your lights and appliances when they are not being used.

There are a few changes you can make around the home that could help cut down your average electricity usage. You can use more efficient gadgets and appliances, from energy-saver lightbulbs to A+++ rated dishwashers, as well as replacing old appliances and avoiding wasted power by switching unused devices off at the plug.

You can upgrade your gas appliances to more efficient models or installing a smart thermostat to help you track usage and have more control over your gas-powered central heating.

Other things you could be doing that will have an impact are:

- turn off all the lights whenever you leave a room
- Turn appliances off at the plug to save.

- You can switch unused appliances on and off via your phone, but you will need to ensure you use specific plug sockets for that. You could also use cheaper timer plugs to schedule turning appliances off.
- Turn down your thermostat by just one degree.
- Upgrade your old boiler to a better energy efficient one
- When the weather is nice outside, open up your windows and use fans around the house to circulate the air and cool down in the summertime.
- Open up your blinds and shade in the winter to allow sunlight in and warm up your home
- When you are cooking, match your pot size to the size of your burner.
- Wash your clothes in colder water, and if you can cut out one wash cycle per week, you will also be clipping money off your energy bill
- Going out of town? Then turn off the water heater.
- Don't leave your electronics on the charger once they are fully charged.
- You can save by washing up in a bowl rather than using a running tap. Use your dishwasher. Dishwashers may use electricity, but they save more energy, money, water, and time than hand washing.

- Buying a more efficient shower head can save you.
- A cold draught can cause your home to lose heat, which in term makes it more tempting to turn the heating up. To prevent this, use draught excluders or draught-proofing kits.
- Seal cracks in floors and skirting boards and block an unused chimney
- Insulate your roof can stop heating from escaping from your home.
- If you don't already have a room thermostat, programmer, and thermostatic radiator valves, installing them could save you money, and it will also cut your home carbon emissions by 320Kg a year.
- If you live in an area where summers are hot, turn on your ceiling fans before you touch your thermostat. Using a ceiling fan can make a room feel 10 degrees cooler, and a fan uses just 10% of the energy than a central air conditioner does.
- If you only need to heat one room in your house, it may be cheaper to use a portable electric heater and keep the thermostat turned down.
- LEDs are the most energy-efficient light bulbs and use almost 90% less energy than traditional incandescents.

- Use motion to stop waste. If you are constantly following family members from room to room, turning off lights behind them, you could use motion detectors.
- Understand your energy bill. It is the first step in knowing how much gas and electricity you are using and where you can cut back.
- Only run your washing machine and dishwasher when they are full, and use energy-efficient programs. Dry your washing outside rather than using your tumble dryer.
- When heating something up or cooking something small, go with a small appliance like your microwave or toaster oven. They use substantially less electricity than your oven.
- Dimming your light reduces wattage and output, which helps save energy.
- The air ducts in your home could be costing you big bucks. Ducks with holes, clogs, and leaks can lose around 20%
- Fix leaky faucets
- Adjust the temperature on your water heater

Another way to save money is by comparing energy quotes. The process is simple - you just need to put in a few details.

Increase your income

There are lots of ways to boost your income or reduce your spending.

Making more money is just as effective as cost-cutting. There are many ways for you to do just that.

Getting a raise - The fastest path to boosting your income. It might be you are ready to grow and be promoted, or you are looking to expand your knowledge with another role. Even if this is not something that can happen immediately, it is worth investing in growing and progressing in your chosen career.

Getting a second job. -You could get a part-time during your off-hours. The additional money can help with your monthly expenses, get out of debt, save more money, and much more. It should not get in the way of your primary income source, though, or ruin your health.

If you can't commit to a part-time then why not add another income stream with a side hustle you do in your spare time? These side gigs offer more flexibility and freedom.

Create a passive income. Do you have a hobby? Have you considered the possibility of making some money out of your hobby?

Passive income is a source of revenue that continues even after the work is complete. Passive income can increase your earnings.

Examples could be a rental property, a limited partnership. As with active income, passive income is usually taxable.

Proponents of earning passive income tend to be boosters of a work-from-home and be-your-own-boss lifestyle. It has been used to define money being earned regularly with little or no effort on the part of the person receiving it.

Don't accept pitiful savings rates. Take action now to ensure you are getting every possible cent of interest on your savings.

An investment ISA/IRA is a great way to save with a chance of getting a good return.

If you put your money in a traditional savings account, then you can predict with certainty what the money will be worth a year down the line.

That is not the case with investing. That is why investing is viewed as a long-term process. It is a really good idea to monitor how those investments are performing on a fair regular basis.

Instead of leaving your money on a savings account, you also might consider investing the money to make it grow, as you will probably make better returns.

Pay off debts with savings. Most people who try to save while in debt are simply throwing their money away. The amount of money you pay in interest to borrow is much more than you earn on your savings, so pay the debt off with savings.

Once you have cleared your debt, you are then free up to save more and faster.

If you have several debts to clear, aim to clear the most expensive ones first.

There are some exceptions where using your savings to pay off your debt may not be cost-effective. If you have money outstanding on an interest-free overdraft or a 0% balance transfer card, these debts will not have higher interest rates than you are earning on your savings. As a result, clearing these is not as urgent.

You should also consider whether you will be charged for clearing your debts early. This is likely the case with your mortgage.

In most cases, clearing your debts before starting to save will make your money go further.

Conclusion

Having a healthy financial situation is as important as any aspects of your life. Especially in this uncertain times we are all living. If you look after your health, your body, why wouldn't you the same with your finances?

After all, if you have very bad finances this will surely affect your mental health and can have serious impact throughout the many areas of your life.

Stop living on credit, buy intentionally, build an emergency fund and stop spending money and start investing it are some of the steps we examined and that will help you on your quest for a better outcome.

The crucial thing to consider is that you willl need to change how you have been acting, some of your habits will need to be adjusted. If you do not change, so won't your results.

This might make you look at important aspects of your life and question them. This is normal and necessary. Passing through life without stop and thinking and making necessary changes will not make your grow, in any aspects.

Have a plan of where you want to go, stick to it and make the necessary changes. The journey may be painful and at times, scary but once you get there, there is nothing like that freedom feeling of being in control and able to direct your life the way your want it.

The change is within your reach…

Other Books By the Author

- *Investment for Beginners (2021)*

- *A Customised Guide for Minimalism (2021)*

www.ingramcontent.com/pod-product-compliance
Lightning Source LLC
Chambersburg PA
CBHW082110220526
45472CB00009B/2129